feline
FRIENDS

Quercus

'Three **little** kittens
They **lost** their **mittens**.'

Eliza Follen, *New Nursery Songs*

'The trouble with a kitten is **that** eventually it becomes a **cat.'** ～ Ogden Nash

'The cat is a dilettante in fur.'

Théophile Gautier

'Pussy cat, pussy cat, where have you been?
I've been in London to look at the queen.
Pussy cat, pussy cat, what did you there?
I frightened a little mouse under her chair.'

Nursery rhyme

'The Cat. He walked by himself, and all places were alike to him.'

Rudyard Kipling, 'The Cat that Walked by Himself'

'Cats are at home everywhere
where one feeds them.'

German proverb

'Yellow cat, black cat, as long as it catches mice, it is a good cat.'

⁓ Deng Xiaoping

'The smallest feline is a masterpiece.'

Leonardo da Vinci

'The cat would eat fish, but would not wet her feet.'

Proverb, 1200s

'You will **always** be lucky
if you know **how** to make
friends with **strange** cats.'

Colonial American proverb

'Oh I am a cat that likes to Gallop about doing good.'

⟞ Stevie Smith, 'The Galloping Cat'

'For he purrs in thankfulness,
when God tells him he's
a good Cat.
For he is an instrument for the children
to learn benevolence upon.'

Christopher Smart, 'My Cat Jeoffrey'

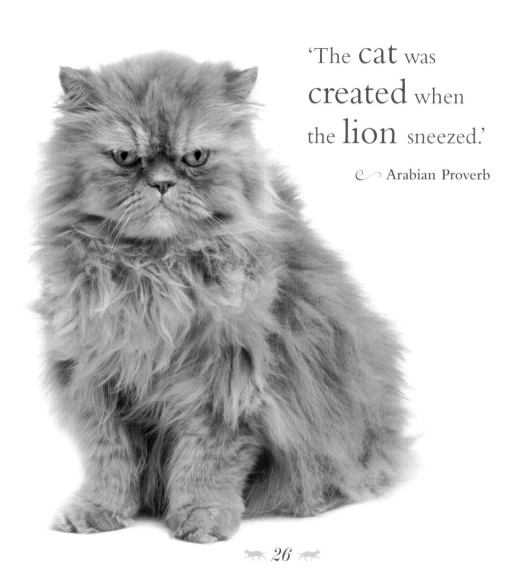

'The cat was created when the lion sneezed.'

⸎ Arabian Proverb

'A cat may look at a king.'

◦ Proverb

'Macavity, Macavity,
there's no one like Macavity,
There never was a Cat of such
deceitfulness and suavity.'

T. S. Eliot, 'Macavity: The Mystery Cat'

'What female heart can gold despise? What cat's averse to fish?'

⌒ Thomas Gray, 'Ode on the Death of a Favourite Cat'

'Mrs Crupp had **indignantly** assured him that there was **not** room to **swing** a cat there; but, as Mr Dick **justly** observed to me, sitting down on the foot of the **bed,** nursing his leg, "You **know,** Trotwood, I don't want to **swing** a cat. I never do **swing** a cat. Therefore, what does that **signify** to me!"'

Charles Dickens, *David Copperfield*

'The Owl looked up to the Stars above

And sang to a small guitar,

'Oh lovely Pussy! O Pussy, my love,

What a beautiful Pussy you are,

You are, You are!

What a beautiful Pussy you are!'

Edward Lear, 'The Owl and the Pussy-Cat'

'It is a very **inconvenient** habit of kittens (Alice had once said) that, **whatever** you say to **kittens**, they always **purr**.'

～ Lewis Carroll, *Through the Looking Glass*

'Tiger Tiger,
burning bright,
In the forests of
the night.'

William Blake, 'The Tiger'

37

'Let some of the tranquillity of the cat Curl into me.'

David Rowbotham, 'The Creature in the Chair'

'In Hans' old Mill his three black cats
Watch the bins for the thieving rats.
Whisker and claw, they crouch in the night,
Their five eyes smouldering green and bright.'

Walter de la Mare, 'Five Eyes' (the three cats are 'Jekkel, and
Jessup, and one-eyed Jill')

41

'I love cats because I love my home, and little by little they become its visible soul.'

⌒ Jean Cocteau, whose cat Karoun wore
a collar inscribed with the words,
'Cocteau belongs to me.'

'A Poet's Cat, sedate and grave
As poet well could wish to have,
Was much addicted to inquire
For nooks to which she might retire,
And where, secure as mouse in chink,
She might repose, or sit and think.'

⟶ William Cowper

'Its tail was a plume of such magnificence that it almost wore the cat.'

⌇ Hugh Leonard, *Rover and Other Cats*

'God invented the cat so that man could have a tiger to stroke at home.'

Victor Hugo

'The greater cats with golden eyes
Stare out between the bars.
Deserts are there, and different skies,
And night with different stars.'

Vita Sackville-West, *The King's Daughter*

'Our perfect companions never have fewer than four feet.'

⟳ Colette

'There are two means of
refuge from the misery of
life – music and cats.'

ℰ Albert Schweitzer

'If animals could speak, the dog would be a blundering outspoken fellow; but the cat would have the rare grace of never saying a word too much.'

℘ Mark Twain

'A cat can be **trusted** to purr when she is **pleased**, which is **more** than can be said for **human** beings.'

William Ralph Inge

'Wanton kittens make sober cats.'

Proverb, 1700s

'I believe cats to be spirits come to earth. A cat, I am sure, could walk on a cloud without coming through.'

e⁀ Jules Verne

'Purring would seem to be . . .
an automatic safety valve
device for dealing with
happiness overflow.'

⌁ Monica Edwards

'The cat is the animal to whom the Creator gave the biggest eye, the softest fur, the most supremely delicate nostrils, a mobile ear, an unrivalled paw and a curved claw borrowed from the rose tree.'

Colette

'It is in the **nature** of cats to do a **certain** amount of **unescorted** roaming.'

℮ Adlai Stevenson

'I have **studied** many **philosophers** and many cats. The **wisdom** of cats is **infinitely** superior.'

e➣ Hippolyte Taine

'A kitten is the most irresistible comedian in the world. Its wide-open eyes gleam with wonder and mirth. It darts madly at nothing at all, and then, as though suddenly checked in the pursuit, prances sideways on its hind legs with ridiculous agility and zeal.'

Agnes Repplier

'Drowsing, they take the noble attitude of a great sphinx, who, in a desert land, sleeps always, dreaming dreams that have no end.'

⁓ Charles Baudelaire, 'The Cat'

'One cat just leads to another.'

Ernest Hemingway – among whose very many cats were Alley Cat, Boise, Crazy Christian, Dillinger, Ecstasy, Fats, Mr Feather Puss, Friendless Brother, Furhouse, Skunk, Thruster, Whitehead and Willy.

'A house **without** a cat, and a **well-fed,** well-petted and properly revered **cat,** may be a **perfect** house, perhaps – but how can it **prove** its title?'

᠆ Mark Twain

'Cats are **mysterious** folk.
There is **more** passing in their
minds than we are **aware** of.'

ᴄ⁓ Sir Walter Scott

'Wherever
a cat sits, there
shall happiness
be first.'

Stanley Spencer

'A little **drowsing** cat is an **image** of **perfect** beatitude.'

∽ Champfleury (Jules Fleury-Husson)

'When I returned home at night, he was pretty sure to be waiting for me near the gate and would rise and saunter along the walk, as though his being there was purely accidental.'

ও Charles Dudley Warner

'Nothing's more playful than a **young** cat, nor more **grave** than an **old** one.'

 Thomas Fuller

'The city of cats and the city of men exist one inside the other, but they are not the same city.'

⌐ Italo Calvino

'The **real** measure of a day's heat is the **length** of a **sleeping** cat.'

෴ Charles J. Brady

'Sometimes he sits at your feet looking into your face with an expression so gentle and caressing that the depth of this gaze startles you. Who can believe that there is no soul behind those luminous eyes!'

Théophile Gautier

'A cat has absolute emotional honesty: human beings, for one reason or another, may hide their feelings, but a cat does not.'

⟶ Ernest Hemingway

'There is **no** more intrepid **explorer** than a **kitten**.'

∾ Champfleury (Jules Fleury-Husson)

'Of all animals, the cat alone attains to the contemplative life. He regards the wheel of existence from without, like the Buddha.'

e~ Andrew Lang

'The eyes of a cat will wax and wane with the phases of the moon.'

— W. B. Yeats

'Cats as a class, have never completely got over the snootiness caused by that fact that in Ancient Egypt they were worshipped as gods.'

P. G. Wodehouse

'A cat's rage is beautiful, burning with pure cat flame, all its hair standing up and crackling blue sparks, eyes blazing and sputtering.'

⌁ William S. Burroughs

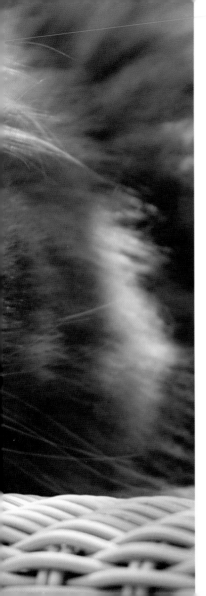

'Both **ardent** lovers and
austere scholars, when
once they come to the
years of **discretion**,
love cats, so **strong** and
gentle, the pride of the
household, **who** like them
are **sensitive** to the **cold**,
and **sedentary**.'

Charles Baudelaire

'Cats always know whether people like or dislike them. They do not always care enough to do anything about it.'

e⌐ Winifred Carriere

'A kitten is a rosebud
in the garden of the
animal kingdom.'

Robert Southey

'Cats are rather delicate creatures and they are subject to a good many different ailments, but I never heard of one who suffered from insomnia.'

e∽ Joseph Wood Krutch

'Most cats, when
they are Out want
to be In, and vice
versa, and often
simultaneously.'

⟨ Louis J. Camuti

'Even if you have just destroyed a Ming Vase, purr. Usually all will be forgiven.'

Lenny Rubenstein

'Kittens are convinced that the whole world is concerned with keeping them entertained.'

F. A. Paradis de Moncrif, *Les Chats*

'The trouble with cats is that they've got no tact.'

⁓ P. G. Wodehouse

'What greater gift than the love of a cat?'

℘ Charles Dickens

First published in Great Britain in 2007 by

Quercus
21 Bloomsbury Square
London
WC1A 2NS

A CIP catalogue record for this book is available from the British Library

ISBN-10: 1 84724 307 X
ISBN-13: 978 1 84724 307 2

Printed and bound in China

10 9 8 7 6 5 4 3

Picture credits: © Pat Doyle/Corbis: p. 6, p. 7, p. 16–17, p. 32, p. 36, p. 37, p. 82, p. 113; © PBNJ Productions/CORBIS: p. 8; © Julie
Habel/CORBIS: p. 10, p. 77; © DK Limited/Corbis: p. 12, p. 13, p. 83, p. 86; © Aaron Horowitz/CORBIS: p.15; © JJorge Ferrari/epa/
Corbis: p. 18; © Frank Lukasseck/Corbis: p. 20; © Herbert Spichtinger/zefa/Corbis: p. 22–3; © Ingrid von Hoff/zefa/Corbis: p. 24, p. 26;
© Lars Christensen/istock: p. 27; © James L. Amos/CORBIS: p. 28; © Image Source/Corbis: p. 30, 72–3; © Dmitry Kosterev/istock: p.
34; © Roy Morsch/CORBIS: p. 38; © Mike Zens/Corbis: p. 40; © Pinto/zefa/Corbis: p. 42, p. 93, p. 110–1; © Marcus Botzek/Corbis:
p. 44, p. 60, p. 114; © Yann Arthus-Bertrand/Corbis: p. 46–7; © Don Mason/Brand X/Corbis: p. 49; © Alexander Hubrich/zefa/Corbis:
p. 50; © Margo Harrison/istock: p. 54; © Vladimir Suponev/istock: p. 52, p. 112 and back cover; © DLILLC/Corbis: p. 56, p. 67; © Scott
T. Smith/CORBIS: p. 58; © Corbis: p. 63, p. 70, p. 81, 104; © Mark A. Johnson/Corbis: p. 64; © M. Rutz/zefa/Corbis: pp. 4–5, p. 68–9;
© Richard Hamilton Smith/CORBIS: p. 74; © Ruediger Knobloch/A.B./zefa/Corbis: p. 78; © Lothar Lenz/zefa/Corbis: p. 84; © Lew
Robertson/Corbis: p. 88–9; © Ron Sanford/Corbis: p. 90; © Hans Strand/CORBIS: p. 94–5; © Simone Neumann/dpa/Corbis: p. 96; ©
Martin Harvey/CORBIS: p. 98; © istock: p. 100; © Henri Caroline/istock: p. 101; © Lisa Klumpp/istock: p. 102–3; © Ed Bock/CORBIS:
p. 106–7; © Myopia/Corbis: p. 108; © ZOE WALTON WEITZ/epa/Corbis: p. 116–7